The Essential George Booth

COMPILED AND EDITED BY LEE LORENZ

WORKMAN PUBLISHING · NEW YORK

A Lee Lorenz Book

For Dione
G.B.

For William Shawn
L.L.

Of the 135 drawings in this collection, 109 originally appeared in *The New Yorker* and were copyrighted © in the years 1969, 1974, and 1976 through 1995 inclusive by The New Yorker Magazine, Inc.

Library of Congress Cataloging-in-Publication Data

Booth, George, 1926–
The essential George Booth / compiled and edited by Lee Lorenz.
p.   cm. — (The essential cartoonists library)
"A Lee Lorenz book."
"A Booth bibliography" : p.163
ISBN 0-7611-1251-0
1. American wit and humor, Pictorial. 2. Booth, George, 1926–
—Interviews. 3. Cartoonists—United States—Interviews.
I. Lorenz, Lee. II. Title. III. Series
NC1429.B6666A4 1998
741.5'973—dc21   98-46586
CIP

Workman books are available at special discounts when purchased in bulk for premiums and sales promotions as well as for fund-raising or educational use. Special editions can also be created to specification. For details, contact the Special Sales Director at the address below.

Workman Publishing Company, Inc.
708 Broadway
New York, NY 10003-9555

Printed in the United States

First printing February 1999
10 9 8 7 6 5 4 3 2 1

"Triple whammy."

"Permission to speak freely, sir!"

PREFACE

George Booth is a tall, loose-jointed gentleman who, when he sported a beard, was often described as "Lincolnesque." (He shaved it off after his father threatened to disown him.)

George describes himself as a "corn belt" Missourian. He was born in Cainsville on June 28, 1926, and grew up in the small town of Fairfax (pop. 800). Booth is a great storyteller. His sense of cadence is impeccable and his punch lines are often preceded, like Jack Benny's, by a seemingly endless pause. His daughter describes this device as "the Missouri Silence." He speaks softly and laughs loudly—especially at his own jokes.

George began drawing "funny pictures" at the age of three and has never stopped. His professional career began in the pages of *Collier's* magazine in 1960. Sales to *Look* and *The Saturday Evening Post* followed, and in 1969 he began appearing regularly in *The New Yorker*. The late James Geraghty, who was then the magazine's art editor, regarded him with awe and bemusement. "Booth is unabashed," he once said. "Occasionally we have to abash him." Today, of course, George is deservedly established as a member of the *New Yorker* pantheon that includes Addams, Thurber, Arno, Hokinson, and Price.

Like all great cartoon humor, Booth's springs from character. Through the years he has created his own repertory company: a tag-sale assortment of cat ladies, plant nuts, eccentrics, misfits, and loners. He records their adventures with affection and a passionate love of detail. Taken together, they constitute a portrait of small-town America as richly realized as the work of his fellow Missourian Mark Twain. Booth is, in fact, a member of that distinguished group of regional American humorists that runs from Twain through Will Rogers and Finley Peter Dunne's "Mr. Dooley" to Herriman's "Krazy Kat" and the early stories of James Thurber.

George Booth is a very talented fellow, but talent is not as rare a commodity as is widely believed. The indispensable ingredients of his success are patience, which he learned from his mother; endurance, which he learned in the Marines; and humility, which he acquired over his eight years as an art director.

A master of protective colorization, Booth works in a modest studio near his home in a quiet corner of suburbia. For diversion, he occasionally drives his vintage car (a cream-colored 1935 Dodge sedan) into town for an ice-cream soda.

He loves music of all kinds and, thanks to his wife, has learned to rejoice in the splendors of nature. They share their home with two cats and enjoy regular visits from their daughter, who works for a large newspaper in a nearby metropolis.

George Booth works hard and sleeps well. He is the rarest kind of artist: a happy man.

—Lee Lorenz

CONTENTS

PREFACE · *vii*

BEGINNINGS · *1*
MOTHER, DAD, AND THE FAMILY • *SUMMER JOB* • *LOST LOVE* •
THE FEW, THE PROUD, THE MARINES • BIG TOWN • PAYING THE RENT •
AT THE NEW YORKER

REPERTORY COMPANY · *38*
MRS. RITTERHOUSE • THE GARAGE • THE STUFF CARTOONS ARE MADE OF •
YARD WORK • LONERS, ODDBALLS, AND MISFITS • *CRIMES OF YOUTH*

CANINES, FELINES, AND BEHEMOTHS · *74*
UPPER CRUST • CAVEMEN

"DEAR MR. BOOTH" · *97*

FARTHER AFIELD · *108*
COMIC STRIPS • ILLUSTRATED BOOKS FOR CHILDREN AND OTHERS •
GREETING CARDS • "DOING THE BATCH"

SHOPTALK · *121*
CAPTIONS • IDEAS • GAGMEN •
SIGHT GAGS • TECHNIQUE • WORK HABITS • INFLUENCES • ADVICE

A BOOTH BIBLIOGRAPHY · *163*

"George Stoner is here from Terre Haute.
He and Henry are talking over old times."

BEGINNINGS

E VERY ARTIST TRACES a different path to *The New Yorker*, but George Booth's has been notable for both its length and its circuitousness. Although George was delighting his parents with "funny pictures" at the age of three, his first cartoon in *The New Yorker* didn't appear until forty years later. In between he was—in order of appearance—the acknowledged "town cartoonist" of Fairfax, Missouri, a printer's devil, a Marine (four hitches), and the editor of a basketful of trade magazines. He spent his free time attending art schools, mastering everything from the basics of layout and design to the intricacies of Tarzan's musculature.

Being a modest man, George Booth freely credits his success to everyone from his first grade teacher to his Marine drill sergeant. At the head of the list, of course, he places his parents.

Main Street, Fairfax, Missouri, Fourth of July, 1939.
Front row: George Booth, far right; brother Gaylord, far left.
Family car, second from right.

1

"Teacher burnout."

MOTHER, DAD, AND THE FAMILY

LORENZ: You always mention your mother as your greatest influence. Tell me about her.

BOOTH: Mother was born in 1903 in the Ozarks. She had three brothers, and one of them, Gaylord, was always drawing cartoons. He died at age twenty-two of tuberculosis, so he was never a professional cartoonist. All my life I heard about Uncle Gaylord—how he just loved to cartoon and be a bit of an imp. So when I began to cartoon, at three, Mother was excited. I drew a racing car stuck in the mud, and I laughed and laughed.

George by Maw Maw.

Mother told me later that she hoped I would continue drawing funny pictures but she wasn't gonna push it, which was probably the correct thing to do. I've been cartooning ever since.

My mother was a teacher. She taught grades one through eight in a one-room schoolhouse in a little town called Lonesome. She'd teach the even grades one year and the odd grades the next year—always the same kids. After she retired, she became a cartoonist and had a regular weekly cartoon in the Princeton, Missouri, *Post-Telegraph Gazette.* She signed it "Maw Maw."

Maw Maw by George.

3

Above: Maw Maw's cartoon strip. Below right: Nature sketch from Maw Maw's notebook.

LORENZ: What was the name of her strip?

BOOTH: She called it "Erfie and Orfie." She also painted portraits—
a lot of them in pastel, a lot of them in oil. At one point, she won
first prize in watercolor in the state of Missouri. She won top prizes in
oil as well.

Mother was an environmentalist way before the rest of the country. They didn't have much where she grew up in the Ozarks, so she
made the most of what she had. She used to "rescue" the wildflow-

SHOOTING MARBLES

HERITAGE

The trees are gone,
The hedges burned,
Old houses buried,
 Fence rows destroyed.

Cruel hand of Man,
You plow and reap,
Spray and poison,—
The beauty you cannot see,
A sacrifice to Greed.

　　　—by my ghost
　　May 7, 1999 A.D.

HELP POIRE OLE MAWMAW
GET NEW TIRES FOR HER
WHEEL CHAIR
THANK YEW!

Sketches, a poem, and a self-portrait from Maw Maw's album.

SUMMER JOB

The summer before I went into the Corps, Dad and I worked together near Harvard, Nebraska. He worked as a union carpenter and I as a laborer. We were building an air base. It was hot, flat country. One almost could not get fired because so many men had gone to war. We had a mean boss named Pete. Dad said Old Pete was a railroad boss. Old Pete would turn red in the face and scream loud, vicious oaths when he spoke to the men. I had never been screamed at by professionals at that point. I was shoving wallboard up to the roofing guys all day long; Dad was doing floors about twenty yards from me. All of a sudden Old Pete was in my face screaming for a hammer. "God dammit! A hammer! A hammer!" I was a quiet kid and had never talked to Old Pete. Dad observed the situation, held his hammer flat, and pitched it the twenty yards so that it landed right at Old Pete's feet. Old Pete was a bit taken aback. If Dad's aim had been a little off, he would have had that hammer in the face. There was silence. Dad walked over and said, "Pete, the boy is stone-deaf . . . can't hear a thing you say." Old Pete went off in a huff, and I worked the rest of the summer without speaking. At times Old Pete would forget and scream at me, but it was of no use.

—G.B.

ers that grew along the railroad tracks and plant them in our backyard. She knew the steam engines would fry them, and she hated to see anything go to waste.

Mother's name was Irma Norene Swindle. She met my dad at Stephens College in Columbia, Missouri. His name was William. William Earl. Earl and Irma. They didn't like those names, so she called him Billy and he called her Bill for the rest of their lives.

Dad was five years older than my mother. He left Cainsville and got an education. Times were hard, and few of his peers did that. He became a schoolteacher and a coach, and he taught Sunday school, too. Later on, he was an administrator for the school system. When he was around sixty, he took a job as supervisor in a town where these big farm boys had more or less taken over their school and stuck the coach's head in a toilet. Dad had done a lot of boxing, and the first day of school he got those boys into the ring as their instructor. Needless to say, discipline was restored.

Silent Night

WM. E. BOOTH

Pap strikes a comic pose for his Christmas card, c. 1950.

Dad knew words. His humor was based on intelligence and integrity—there was no room for the vulgar. Once my kid brother dug up a pipe by the back door. When he was finished, the fresh dirt was the shape of a tiny grave. People came to the farm for various reasons, and when they asked about the grave smack up to the back door Dad would explain, "Old Tom is buried there."

We called our dad "Dad" or "Daddy," although I wrote him as "Pap"—that was kind of between me and him. I have two brothers. Gaylord is two years older than me; Jim is four years younger. When Gaylord was fourteen, he had a BB rifle. One day, he was on the porch about thirty yards from where Dad and I were talking, and he hauled off and shot Dad in the arm of his jacket. When Dad asked him what he thought he was doing, Gaylord said, "I was trying to hit George."

George, Gaylord, Jim, and Maw Maw.

LORENZ: Where are your brothers now?

BOOTH: Gaylord is living in Arizona and Jim lives in Springfield, Missouri, which is in the Ozarks. We're a close-knit family. When people ask me do I

"One of you boys go help Mom with the groceries."

still have family in Missouri, I just have to tell 'em that they're mostly either dead or captured by this time.

LORENZ: At what point did you decide you wanted to be a cartoonist or an artist of some kind?

BOOTH: Age three. When I was six or seven, I was trying comic strips. I did a comic strip called "Cherokee Cherky." I thought it was funny.

LORENZ: Is Cherky meant to be Turkey?

BOOTH: I don't know what my reasoning was. We're part Cherokee on my mother's side, and that fascinated me. There was an ancestor on the Trail of Tears. His name was Fly.

I went to a school in Fairfax and drew all the time. Mother and I both painted signs. A truck-door name and town cost one dollar per door. I painted the doors on a semi-trailer cattle truck, put it in the wrong gear to back out of the building, went forward, and loosened the wall pretty good. My whole family supported my career. When I was sixteen, Dad insisted that I learn something else so I could eat. I became a printer's devil. That was good advice because in years to come I operated the linotype at night after school in Chicago and later at the naval base in Pearl Harbor after V-J Day.

As the school administrator, Dad was instrumental in putting out the school newspaper, so of course I went to work drawing cartoons. I also worked on the local newspaper, the Fairfax *Forum,* when I was still in high school. We put out two weekly newspapers. The other one was for Watson, Missouri, and I would draw for both of them. I became the town cartoonist.

Facing page: This drawing includes, at the left, a linotype machine of the type George wrestled with as a teenage apprentice.

10

"*Correction: The obituary for 'Ta Ta' Bottorff appearing in the November 12th edition of the Post-News and Gazette-Telegraph incorrectly listed 'Ebbie' Bottorff, of Spickert, as the son of 'Ta Ta' Bottorff. 'Ebbie' Bottorff is the brother of 'Ta Ta' Bottorff, and also we are pleased to say that both 'Ta Ta' Bottorff and 'Ebbie' Bottorff are living and in good health. The Post-News and Gazette-Telegraph regrets the error.*"

LOST LOVE

When I was in my early twenties, my folks and I went to Tuscumbia, Missouri. They had business. Upper Tuscumbia sits on the top of the Osage River bluff, then directly all the way down the bluff is Lower Tuscumbia. The folks were in the bank and I was in the car at Lower Tuscumbia, which was one store–restaurant–pool hall. A beautiful young girl with long black hair rode up bareback and tied her horse to the hitching rail. She went in the store and sat at the counter next to an old man in overalls. I followed and sat on the other side of the girl. It was true love. I noticed a callus on her right middle finger like the one I get from holding a pen. I asked her if she was an artist. She said, "No." I explained that I noticed the callus on her finger and it was like the ones that artists sometimes develop.

The old man in overalls was evidently deaf. He shouted to the girl, "What does he want?" She shouted back, "He's asking me about my wart!" The old man leaned back to get a clear look at me. I spilled my coffee a little and left.

—G.B.

THE FEW, THE PROUD, THE MARINES

There is little about the affable and indifferently attired Mr. Booth to suggest the tough spit-shine image of the U.S. Marines. The only visible residue of his four hitches, eight years, is a firm handshake and good posture. The true legacy, of course, is his career as a comic artist.

Booth joined the Marines right out of high school. His prolonged tour of duty was spent primarily producing drawings, spots, and illustrations as well as cartoons for *Leatherneck*, the Marine Corps magazine. Booth credits his education as an artist to the generosity of his *Leatherneck* editors and fellow staff contributors. In addition, while stationed in Washington, D.C., and later in Chicago, he had the opportunity to fine-tune his skills at some of the best art schools in the country. George Booth may not be the Marines' first choice as a poster boy, but the pleasure his work has given to millions of Americans does make a strong case for "your tax dollars at work."

BOOTH: The war was on, and in 1944 I joined the Marines. My brother had joined the Air Corps, which he considered number one. The Marines were number two. I joined the Fourth Marine Division, based on Maui, but I didn't get into combat. I was a replacement for the guys coming back from Iwo Jima, but by then the war was over and everybody was going home. I got a letter from Washington saying that I could come back to D.C. and be on the staff of *Leatherneck*, provided I would reenlist. I thought about that pretty hard, because I didn't like the Marine Corps very much at that point. I did reenlist, and it was a great opportunity. I joined *Leatherneck* in 1946.

The drawings on the facing page are from "Shook Up," Booth's regular feature in *Leatherneck*. Clearly Booth the stylist has not yet emerged, but the idea of a Marine going nose to nose with a gopher in a foxhole is vintage Booth.

shook up

BY BOOTH

"What's the password?"

"Artillery position, six hundred yards, north by northeast, six men—looks like they're preparing to . . ."

"Knocked myself out for yesterday's inspection . . . you didn't even show up.
Today I decided to hell with it . . . and here you are bigger'n sin!"

LORENZ: And that was based in Washington?

BOOTH: Correct. I did cartoons and spots, and then, in January of '47, I had a full-color cover. I did pages and spreads, and they played up my name. That's how I got started. I'm grateful it worked.

LORENZ: This was a two-year reenlistment?

BOOTH: Yes. The art director at *Leatherneck* was a civilian, Don Margo, who had previously been art director of *Esquire*. We were in uniform in Washington, D.C., but on subsistence pay. I was so happy about the opportunity that I would often sleep in the art department. Later, I rented a cheap room for twenty-eight dollars a month near the Smithsonian. I spent most of my money eating in a Chinese restaurant and at cafeterias. I was hypnotized by cafeterias. At any rate, I was in print in a national, worldwide, slick magazine. When Mother handed her blind mother a copy of the magazine that had my stuff in it, Grandma felt it carefully and said, "Why, it's not a pulp magazine."

In 1950, I was called up for the Korean War and went through basic training again, but I got sent back to Washington instead of going to the First Division in Korea. So I had another chance at cartooning, back at *Leatherneck*, in 1951 and early '52. In '51 I broke into *Collier's*. Gurney Williams, the cartoon editor there, wrote me a letter. John Bailey, of the *Post*, wrote me a letter, too, and asked me to submit ideas.

LORENZ: Had they seen your work in *Leatherneck*?

BOOTH: I did a cover that caught their attention. It was a line drawing of one Marine down in the corner swinging his rifle by the barrel and scattering Koreans and Chinese all over the cover; everything was flying away. And some guy wrote in and said you've got everything in there but the kitchen sink. The editors wrote back and said, "Look closely, the kitchen sink is in there." Anyway, that cover caught people's attention. I even got a note from Milton Caniff.

LORENZ: So you were well launched.

Near right: The first appearance of what became the typical Booth cat. Facing page: Full cover, with kitchen sink in top right-hand corner.

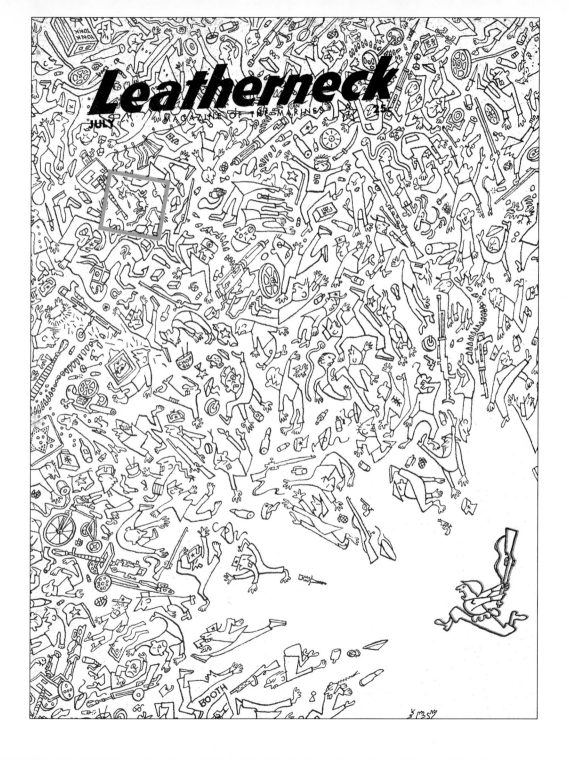

BIG TOWN

BOOTH: I thought I had it made. I came to New York in '52, after I finally got discharged, and went to the School of Visual Arts on the G.I. Bill. I cherished the class in anatomy with Burne Hogarth, the illustrator of Tarzan. It was fascinating to watch him create a figure by laying on one muscle at a time. When he put it all together, he had the "Lord of the Jungle." The cartoon advertising classes were also interesting because of the logic and layout.

LORENZ: You had already received some overtures from *Collier's* and *The Saturday Evening Post*. How did it go?

BOOTH: At first I just beat the pavements. I sold spots. I did two editorial jobs, one for a candy publication and one for a soft drink publication. Mistakenly, I didn't trust anybody. I'd make a deal with them, fifteen dollars a cartoon, and I would hand them the finished cartoon when they handed me the check. Gradually I started making the rounds of the popular magazines. I went to *The Saturday Evening Post, Collier's,* and others. I met Charlie Schulz. He was at *The Saturday Evening Post*. He started his "Peanuts" thing about then. I met Mort Walker by going to a party. Mort comes from Missouri, too. And so does Fred Lasswell, who did "Snuffy Smith." I met *The New Yorker*'s Otto Soglow, an excellent cartoonist, who created "The Little King." He was not much over four feet tall himself. Every time there was a formal gathering of cartoonists, somehow it was required that Otto get up and make a report. He would get up with papers ready. Then all the guys would start shouting for Otto to please stand up. He *was* standing up.

One of Booth's early sales to *Look*
(March 8, 1955).

"Mercy sakes! Look at all the guns and knives and stuff!"

Early on, I won a contest with United Features and did a syndicated panel that lasted one year. It was about a dog called Spot who thought he was a person. It got a lot of reaction but didn't last.

LORENZ: What happened to it?

BOOTH: It died. That was around 1954 or '55.

PAYING THE RENT

BOOTH: As a result of my work on *Leatherneck,* I knew a lot about layout and design. After I got married, in 1958, I wasn't making enough freelance to keep us going, so I took a job as art director with Bill Communications. They had nine trade magazines, such as *Tide* magazine. I would have cartoons in all of them all the time, and occasional covers. Slides for salesmen, brochures, promotional stuff, I did that, too. I was a one-man art department.

LORENZ: Did you have time to continue your cartooning outside?

BOOTH: No, I didn't. But I did a lot of cartooning with the trade publications. I got a lot of experience there, and I learned most of it from the printing salesmen and the people who would volunteer information.

LORENZ: So you learned a lot about the business side of things.

BOOTH: Yes. I also hired guys and gals from the School of Visual Arts and Pratt. I would put one student over in a corner and give him a magazine with a four-color cover and let him do it. Then I'd hire another one and put her in a different corner, and I'd tell this one, you learn from that guy, because I didn't know what to tell 'em. And it worked. But I didn't want to stay forever. I wanted to cartoon.

LORENZ: Did you have any luck selling to *The New Yorker* at that time?

BOOTH: No. I would try periodically. I used to paper my walls with the rejection slips. When they returned my submissions and left out the rejection slip, I was disappointed. It got so I never expected a sale.

LORENZ: Who were your *New Yorker* favorites?

BOOTH: Sam Cobean was outstanding. George Price, Charles Addams, Alain, Helen Hokinson, Mary Petty, all the old-timers. I thought about it and decided I had to break away from Bill Communications and go after *The New Yorker*. I got serious. I started submitting regularly. That was in '58.

LORENZ: So how did you finally break free?

BOOTH: I quit.

LORENZ: Was that a leap of faith, or were you beginning to sell?

Vintage rejection slips from the artist's extensive collection.

TRUE

the man's magazine

67 WEST FORTY-FOURTH STREET, NEW YORK 18, N.Y.

Dear Contributor:

Sorry, but we cannot use the enclosed roughs. Thanks anyhow for letting us see them.

The Philadelphia Inquirer

Philadelphia 1

June 21, 1950.

Mr. George W. Booth,
5842 North Sheridan Road,
Chicago 40, Illinois.

Dear Mr. Booth:

We thank you for having submitted the ten cartoons with a view to publication in TODAY.

However, we are sorry that we cannot make a selection from this group and are, therefore, returning the cartoons to you herewith.

KING FEATURES SYNDICATE

235 East 45th Street

New York 17, N. Y.

The Editors of Kings Features Syndicate regret to say that at this time we cannot use the cartoon roughs which you submitted for publication. However, we hope that you will try us again.

Thank you.

23

Sketches from an unsold strip (1955).

BOOTH: I asked the boss for more money and we couldn't reach an agreement, so I gave a year's notice and held to it. I didn't burn my bridges, though. I did a lot of work for the company on a retainer basis, which was very nice because I knew everybody there and I knew what they wanted. They were kind to me.

LORENZ: Were you living downtown then?

BOOTH: Yes, Dione and I had an apartment on West Twenty-Second Street, and later on West Eleventh Street in the Village, which was lovely. And we lived in Brooklyn Heights for a year or so. We moved out to Long Island

twenty-nine years ago. Our daughter, Sarah, was six months old, and we've been there ever since.

LORENZ: Although everyone associates you with *The New Yorker*, your first big break was with *Collier's* and *The Saturday Evening Post*.

BOOTH: In 1966, Charley Barsotti started his feature "My Kind of People" in the *Post*. I admired his stuff, and when he took over as cartoon editor a year later, I wrote him a note that said, "My wife Dione and I like your work, and we think you'll like mine." He invited me in, one Wednesday afternoon after all the other artists had left, and we hit it off right away. Anyway, Charley gave Mr. Emerson, who was the editor, a hard sell on me, and they decided to run a four-page spread of my stuff. It was a big deal for me, so I wanted to do the layout myself.

LORENZ: I don't remember seeing that.

BOOTH: You didn't. The week before I brought it in, the magazine folded.

LORENZ: Oh, man.

BOOTH: Yeah, well, things worked out. It seems Mr. Shawn, the editor of *The New Yorker,* called Mr. Emerson to offer his sympathy, and Emerson asked him to take a look at my work and the work of Charley Barsotti.

LORENZ: Really?

BOOTH: That's the truth. That was in 1969. I met Jim Geraghty, who was the cartoon editor, and Frank Modell, his assistant. It was real nice.

LORENZ: Did you start selling right away?

BOOTH: Well, no, not right away. Here's what happened: I was attempting to draw *New Yorker* cartoons. They didn't want that because they were already getting that from their regulars. I didn't realize what I was doing until I caught myself laughing at stuff I was sending somebody in a letter. I started doing what I thought was funny, and Geraghty and Mr. Shawn caught it right away. They liked it because it was not what they had. Then I had a start.

Facing page: When George showed this cartoon to Barsotti, it sort of scared him out of his chair. A year later, Booth showed it to Jim Geraghty at *The New Yorker,* and he threw a fit, too. About thirty years after that, he showed it to us at *The New Yorker* and we bought it.

AT THE NEW YORKER

Under the editorship of William Shawn (1951–1987), *The New Yorker* developed a somewhat undeserved reputation for prudishness. During the social upheavals of the sixties, while other publications were gleefully replacing the asterisks in s**t and f**k, the magazine stuck to its tradition of avoiding "street language." More than anything else, this attitude flowed from Shawn's reluctance to seem "trendy." There was a higher priority, however —the search for the perfectly appropriate phrase. After two weeks of considering alternatives, Shawn agreed to let "Whistle, you dumb bastard!" run as submitted.

The skies did not fall, although one outraged mother did write to complain that her eleven-year-old daughter, coming on the caption unexpectedly, suffered "a severe tummy-ache."

"Whistle, you dumb bastard!"

"He did O.K. until the hot-towel shampoo, then he went all to pieces."

"Your mother eats all the wrong foods."

"*While you were on vacation, Zooker, a motion was made and seconded to saw five and a half inches off your chair legs.*"

"*My fellow-employees, it is my painful duty to tell you that discovery of a cash shortage was made this morning amounting to some eighteen million dollars.*"

"The Hewletts have flaming crown roast au vin blanc every Wednesday."

"There is a man at the door who needs seventeen dollars to buy some sweet grass
to burn as a spiritual cleansing agent during his prayer ceremonies."

"It's time to bring in the wax begonias and your mother."

*"I leave messages in the pussycats' little voice-mail boxes.
Sometimes they get back to me. Sometimes they don't."*

REPERTORY COMPANY

THE BEST COMIC ARTISTS create their own cast of characters. Some, like the Addams Family, become household names. Others enter the language as a kind of shorthand for familiar types: Thurber's men, Arno's bimbos, Hokinson's matrons, Saxon's suburbanites. And, of course, Booth's cats and dogs. Few artists have developed a repertory as extensive as Mr. Booth's. The amateur orchestras, Mr. Pudney, breeder of miniature horses, and the assorted misfits are clearly drawn from originals in his hometown. The cavemen are a chance to exercise the mastery of anatomy that he gained in the classes of Tarzan illustrator Burne Hogarth.

Undoubtedly Booth's most popular creation is the redoubtable Mrs. Ritterhouse.

MRS. RITTERHOUSE

LORENZ: Is Mrs. Ritterhouse based on a real person?

BOOTH: Mother.

LORENZ: Did she also play with an amateur orchestra?

BOOTH: Off and on. She was a violinist, pianist, and singer, and she played the Jew's harp and banjo. She used to play "When the Saints Go Marching In" with a lot of energy while bouncing up and down on the piano bench.

"From the top—'Watermelon Man.'
Let's sock it out and give Mrs. Ritterhouse a chance to really cook!"

"Rehearsal's off! Our first violinist was apprehended early this morning poaching clams in Great South Bay! The authorities have confiscated her rake and long tongs!"

"Now, last time, near the end of Ravel's 'Bolero,' I heard a scream."

"Take it from the beginning. Act One. 'Gypsy.' 'May We Entertain You?'
And this time, Mrs Ritterhouse, <u>without</u> the Baby June split."

"There are few moments in music so thrilling as when Brucie and Mrs. Ritterhouse start riffing in tandem."

THE GARAGE

George Booth is to the corner garage what John Philip Sousa is to the Stars and Stripes. Long before *The New Yorker* started accepting scratch-and-sniff advertising, the magazine would occasionally exude a peculiar but unmistakable scent—a combination of crankcase oil, rotting upholstery, and unwashed dog, announcing that the issue contained a drawing of Mr. Booth's inimitable garage.

LORENZ: The garage is one of your favorite settings. Is it real?

BOOTH: It sure is. Lee Murphy and I used to hang out in Bohaty's garage in Centerport, Long Island, before I was married. We both drove Model A Fords. I paid fifty bucks for mine and ninety dollars a year for insurance because it was an antique. And to keep my fifty-dollar car running I had to . . .

LORENZ: . . . spend a lot of time in the garage.

BOOTH: That's right. Make friends. And I observed the things in the garage, which were American—about as American as you can get.

LORENZ: And Mr. Bohaty kept you running.

BOOTH: Yes. He's passed on now, but he was a fine person.

LORENZ: Who is Mr. Ferguson?

BOOTH: I became friends with a Mr. Ferguson *after* I started this Ferguson thing. One of the first cartoons I did for Jim Geraghty used the name Ferguson. And he let me know that he and William Shawn were amused by that name. I never learned why, but I kept on using it.

Al, the owner of Al's Auto Lubrication & Tune-Up, is so pleased with his little joke he has to hold his belly.

"If I were a surgeon, Mr. Ferguson, which I ain't, and your car was my patient, which it ain't—except that it is, in a funny sort of way; that is, if you want to look at it like that; you know what I mean—and you was her husband, I'd have to say, 'Sir, your wife is going to need a valve job.'"

"Murchison's theory is that it's dog hair in your fuel line."

*"We located the hissing noise, Mr. Watkins.
Your wife's mother is in the back seat."*

"That metallic grinding means her throwout bearings are shot.
She's backfiring through her carburetor. The tick indicates transmission trouble,
and the smoke means she's on fire."

"Jesse, isn't that one of Mr. Ferguson's wheels?"

"Nap time."

"Wendel found an Israeli tomato stuck in your front water hose."

THE STUFF CARTOONS ARE MADE OF

The Saturday morning assault on flea markets, yard sales, and just plain old junk sales is a way of life for Americans of every economic station. Booth's lovingly detailed documentation of these phenomena begins, of course, with the familiar cluttered farmyards of his youth, full of rusting tools and broken furniture. But he's equally good at recording the detritus of middle-class suburbia, and even the rare treasures to be harvested from the bottom of the harbor.

LORENZ: I know you enjoy drawing the real thing. Nothing is made up.

BOOTH: Right. George Price would fill a house full of stuff. I examined his work closely, and I could see that everything was placed very carefully— it was never just junk. I sketch directly from yard sales. Then I take out the parts I like and reassemble them.

LORENZ: The objects in your drawings, and in Price's, also help to reveal character. It tells you something about all those people who buy and sell this stuff.

BOOTH: Charles Addams, who studied architecture, knew how to create a stage setting. He was marvelous. I do a little bit of that. It's all north Missouri that you're seeing, but it's really no different from New York. People identify with it. The antiques, the guy sitting in the chair, the little piece of furniture with the lamp on it. That's from going to antique shops and junk stores and garage sales. My mother-in-law has one of those lamps, and it's human interest.

LORENZ: People feel you're paying attention.

BOOTH: Well, they feel—hey, we have one of those, my grandmother had one of those. And that's a warm thing, as opposed to drawing a stock setting with a cartoon chair and a cartoon lamp. Nobody cares about that.

"He married her for her stuff."

"There's more inside."

"Oh, <u>good!</u> Lucille is sending me some stuff!"

"No doubt about it. Scientifically speaking, knowledge of the river will expand in direct proportion to the length of Mr. Van Gundy's new air hose."

"The way I see it, Wendy, you only go around once."

"*That, honey, is probably an end.*"

YARD WORK

My daughter didn't know daddies went to work when she was growing up. I worked in my backyard studio, a rebuilt garage with Dione's greenhouse attached. One morning, when she was about fourteen, my daughter went off to school a few blocks away. Help was needed in the yard. I don't always function well out of cartooning. I pulled a stretch skirt off the clothesline, stuffed a pillow in my shirt, and tied a babushka over my head. I was wearing boots and had a beard. Eventually I was around in the little front yard, raking and singing. One of my daughter's male teachers jogged by and said, "Good morning, Mister Booth." When my daughter came home, she said, "Daaaad! It's all over school that you're a transvestite!"

—G.B.

LONERS, ODDBALLS, AND MISFITS

Booth has produced a remarkable series of loners, and the reader can laugh at them comfortably because they present themselves entirely free of self-pity. The lady in the cap may get her two days on the Orient Express, but the experience will only join other equally valued memorabilia— old band records and a no-longer-wearable set of dancing pumps under the bed. Whether the woman in the cap is related to, or even the same person as, Leon's companion is a question that Mr. Booth refuses to answer. He does acknowledge, however, that Leon's friend is named "Youbetcha."

Cartooning is a lonely profession, so it's hardly surprising that the soliloquy is as common a device among comic artists as the traditional two guys in a saloon. The best caption often seems snipped from that ongoing monologue that buzzes in your head as you sit chewing on a pencil and staring at a blank sheet of paper.

Booth never gave a name to the bachelor with the dog. As he says, "The guy didn't have any friends, so he didn't need a name."

"*Each to each, I always say! Share and share alike! I take pride in my cuisine,*
but at the same time I am willing to divvy up household chores with a wife.
Say, a wife named Irma. That is, if Irma shares as breadwinner! I'll do the cooking!
We'll split the cleaning and the shopping right down the middle!
Irma, you feed the dog! And help yourself to some more turnips."

"The question, Leon, is: What is man?"

"This is a night for white wine."

"There's lots of things in my life I absolutely needed to put in, and now there's lots of things in my life I absolutely need to get out."

CRIMES OF YOUTH

A guy sent me a letter with one of my drawings from The New Yorker. *It was a drawing of the lady in the baseball cap talking to her dog. On the floor were a box of tacks and a hammer, and she had driven some of the tacks into the floor. He circled that part of the drawing and wrote, "What in hell is this?" Well, when I was a kid I once found a hammer and a box of nails in the living room and I did just that same thing. I didn't write back and tell him, though. I was afraid he'd think I was crazy.*

—G.B.

"I want two days and one dazzling night on the Orient Express!"

The New Yorker encouraged Booth to continue his "Man in the Tub" as a series—a latter-day evocation of Price's memorable Floating Man of the early thirties. "We got a pretty good run out of it," says Booth. "In one drawing, I managed to get in eighty-six cats, my all-time record. Eventually, I even got a cover out of it."

"How about supper in the tub tonight, hon?"

"Harry, I wish you'd stop singing 'The Impossible Dream' and help me feed the pussies once in a while."

"Putty took a wife. Her name was Pussums, and she bore him Little Gentleman, Biddy Boo, Savor Tooth, Fluffy, Harry Cat, and Caesar. Then Little Gentleman begat Little Gentleman II and Friday and Twinkle Toes and Possum Tail and . . ."

"How would I rate, hon, on a scale of one to ten?"

Although George's art is deeply rooted in his own experience, his references, to protect the innocent, are deliberately oblique. A rare exception is his "House Plant" series. Although George's wife, Dione, looks even less like the shrewish wife than George (six-foot-three in his stocking feet) looks like the long-suffering husband, the setting is based directly on the Booth living room. "That room looked familiar to me," says George, "but I didn't recognize it until I started putting in the staircase on the right."

"I decided to spend the money and have my legs waxed."

"Remember the Babylonian ziggurat?"

"The cat is out late tonight, but don't worry about it.
She'll come home pretty soon."

"Who has pink eyes, long ears, a cute little cotton tail,
and brings baskets of eggs on Easter morning?"

CANINES, FELINES,
AND BEHEMOTHS

ABOY AND HIS DOG go together like hot dogs and baseball. To discover that George Booth, the supreme chronicler of dogs in our time, never had a pooch of his own is like learning that Norman Rockwell had never tasted apple pie. In fact, George grew up in a typical farm community where dogs and cats were considered yard animals, not pets. Like everyone else, they had to earn their keep. The cats kept the mice out of the barn and the basement. The dogs kept the foxes out of the henhouse and the raccoons out of the grain bins. Not surprisingly, then, Booth's cats

and dogs are more apt to display the peevish independence of the hired hand than the docile servility of household pets.

LORENZ: Let's talk about dogs.

BOOTH: I did a cartoon of the Schoonover sisters, two old ladies who looked exactly alike, sitting with a bunch of other ladies at a quilting bee. A couple of the other ladies are talking, and one of them says, "The Schoonover sisters' cotton batting is loose." And some woman wrote me a letter. She ignored the gag, which I thought was funny. Instead, she said, "I just love that little dog sitting underneath the quilt on the right," and she carried on in the letter about that little dog. So I started drawing more dogs.

LORENZ: What kind of dog did you draw?

BOOTH: Well, I drew the ugliest-looking mutt I could draw, and a fan wrote in on that, too, and asked what is that—an English bullterrier? I didn't know what one was, so I went to the library and looked it up.

LORENZ: And was he an English bullterrier?

BOOTH: He was heading in that direction.

LORENZ: What is the direction of your cats?

BOOTH: In Missouri a cat doesn't come in the house. Nor a dog, for that matter. They're barnyard animals. I never was very close to cats. Dione got me started on them.

LORENZ: So you got the cats by marriage.

BOOTH: Yes, we've always had a house full of cats. A cat will be a spotted Indian pony, or a hippopotamus, or a mule, or wherever he's at that day. Strange. And they'll be a dog, too; that's where my dogs come from. Looking at the back of a dog, actually it's a cat that I see—you know, that I experience.

LORENZ: But dogs are always only dogs, right? They don't play these various roles like cats.

BOOTH: I'm saying, I put the same thing into the dogs that I see in cats, and of course I observe dogs everywhere. I have a feeling for them. A monk in upstate New York sent me a paper he'd written that classified me as a dog expert.

LORENZ: In terms of the psychology of dogs?

BOOTH: Well, I've never had any clinical experience, really. Book experience. Observation.

"Write about dogs!"

"I feed the cat nothing but veggies."

"Let's swap some cats today."

"Edgar, please run down to the shopping center right away, and get some milk and cat food. Don't get canned tuna, or chicken, or liver, or any of those awful combinations. Shop around and get a surprise. The pussies like surprises."

"Once it catches on, the small-horse household-pet idea will go like blazes.
And you may quote Mr. Pudney on that."

"It seems some days like I make a little progress, then other days
it seems like I'm not getting anywhere at all."

UPPER CRUST

Although George Booth has drawn his share of clubmen and plutocrats, the subjects closest to his heart clearly reflect the world he grew up in: decent, hardworking, middle-class folks, struggling to keep up. Occasionally, perhaps to keep his eye fresh, he explores less familiar territory. As imagined by Booth, the antics of the upper crust are as remote, and hilarious, as the doings of the proto-humans of the lower Paleolithic.

LORENZ: Most of your material is at the lower end of the social scale, but every once in a while you do something upscale.

BOOTH: Yeah, clean the place up. There are days when I hear a snap of uncouplement from this level of life, but then I remember those great movies from the thirties and forties. They're like Arno's cartoons. Everyone wears tuxedos and they usually have a cocktail in hand.

LORENZ: The butler in the "Biggers" drawing seems out of place. He goes with the house, not with the people.

BOOTH: He's not real happy to be there, but he has to have a job. He's a Boris Karloff, and I had had him or a butler like him in another scene where he was talking to a horse.

LORENZ: And the horse has this big smile on his face.

"Biggers, two more Luau Sizzlers for Annie and me and another
Fog Cutter for Mrs. Grindstaff."

BOOTH: A horse with an English saddle, you know, that's money, and the butler is money and the place is money, and it's a different kind of nuttiness than you see in those junk places. It wouldn't be so funny to have a horse there, because everything's crazy anyway. It's funnier with the grand piano and the money.

"He's nuts. She's nuts. All three young ones are nuts. The dog is nuts. And the old lady upstairs is nuts, too."

"*All Vangundy is or ever shall be he owes to his mother.*"

"Would you see to old Peterson? He's in the philodendron again."

"Mr. Blanny has suggested that, this being almost September, and he finished late getting the storm windows in place, perhaps it would give us a chance to catch up if we skipped replacing them with the screens and go right into winter with the storm windows already in place just this one time."

CAVEMEN

LORENZ: I love your proto-humans with the big calluses on their behinds.

BOOTH: I do, too. I love to draw them.

LORENZ: Where did you get the idea for the calluses?

BOOTH: Just the fact that they sit down. You know, it gets like that. Here's where the anatomy I studied paid off.

LORENZ: Yeah, Burne Hogarth would be proud of you.

BOOTH: I don't think of these guys as made up. Reality is terribly important. These guys are real. I saw one this morning on the Avenue of the Americas.

"Research and development."

"We may as well go home. It's obvious that this meeting
isn't going to settle anything."

"Yee yee hee hee haw haw yip yip!"

"Yee yee hee hee haw haw yip yip!"

"You seem depressed."

"Put the cat out and come to bed."

"Will your mother be coming down for dinner tonight?"

"*Messenger, dost thou bring me good news or dost thou bring me bad news?*"

"DEAR MR. BOOTH"

JAMES THURBER ONCE COMPLAINED that the drawings for which he was most frequently praised invariably turned out to have been done by William Steig. Grousing about this lack of recognition is endemic among cartoonists, but the evidence suggests that they secretly cherish their anonymity. (How many cartoonists have legible signatures?) Certainly their chosen mode of expression keeps the audience at a distance. Each drawing is launched with high hopes and low expectations—a note in a bottle cast into the sea. The occasional response is usually of the "What's funny about that?" variety.

Mr. Booth is a rare exception to this dreary scenario. Readers identify deeply with his work, and are often moved to write and tell him so. Among George's many admirable traits is the alacrity with which he answers his fan mail. Even so, the response generated by his January 1975 spread "IP GISSA GUL" blew a hole in his working life from which he is still struggling to recover.

LORENZ: We received so many letters about "IP" at *The New Yorker*. One guy even set it to music and had it sung by the church choir. How did you come up with this idea?

BOOTH: The thing I remember about this cartoon was, I went on vacation with Dione's family in New Hampshire. We rented a country house up there. And one way for me to relax and be happy is to sit down and work. So I took my dictionary and thesaurus.

"College teachers have used this cartoon as part of their instruction, and I'm not sure I understand that. Another guy (I think he was a psychiatrist) wrote two pages of solid typewritten copy explaining what I meant. It interested me, because I didn't know any of that."

—G.B.

LORENZ: Is the dictionary one of your regular tools?

BOOTH: Yes, and my light table, I can't breathe without that stuff. An Oxford dictionary, too, and now a Yiddish dictionary. It grows . . .

LORENZ: Why a Yiddish dictionary?

BOOTH: Because Yiddish words pertain more and more—words that I can't find in a regular dictionary. And Jewish humor, along with humor in the movie industry and vaudeville, is part of our culture. It's just fantastic. Anyway, I got up there in the woods and I wanted to do something without

any boundaries. I like to draw early people, so I sat down and started doodling, and it turned into a comic strip. I roughed something out, and then it had the need of a language, so I had to have a language evolve. I tried to keep the freedom, and not edit, and that meant using the word "ass" instead of "that's."

I thought that would kill this thing for you guys, but I submitted it to *The New Yorker* anyway and you didn't kill anything. I think you made one or two little changes and said you'd run it. That was a thrill for me because I really didn't expect you to take it.

BOOTH: People write when you touch them personally. For instance, there are musical groups all over the country that feel very strongly about what they do. If you make a cartoon about them, they'll respond. Saxophone players in particular respond. I once got a check for five dollars from the World Saxophone Congress as a thank-you for a full page I drew. That was amazing. I started getting letters from saxophone players. I got a letter from the Salvation Army with a picture of their saxophone player who was retiring— they wanted me to do something for him.

"I'm in a bit of a rush this morning. May I have just the shoeshine?"

"How often, might I ask, does the World Saxophone Congress meet?"

Not all of George's mail is favorable. After the appearance of this spread, featuring fuel-efficient, environmentally friendly vehicles propelled by dog power, a clutch of outraged readers wrote to accuse him of animal abuse. (One renounced him as a "closet vivisectionist.")

KEEPING GOING

New York City Twenty-dog bus

NEW YORK CITY 20·DOG BUS

Three-dog runabout

details of brake

Dogs answering to "Gee!" and "Haw!" are preferable to steering harness

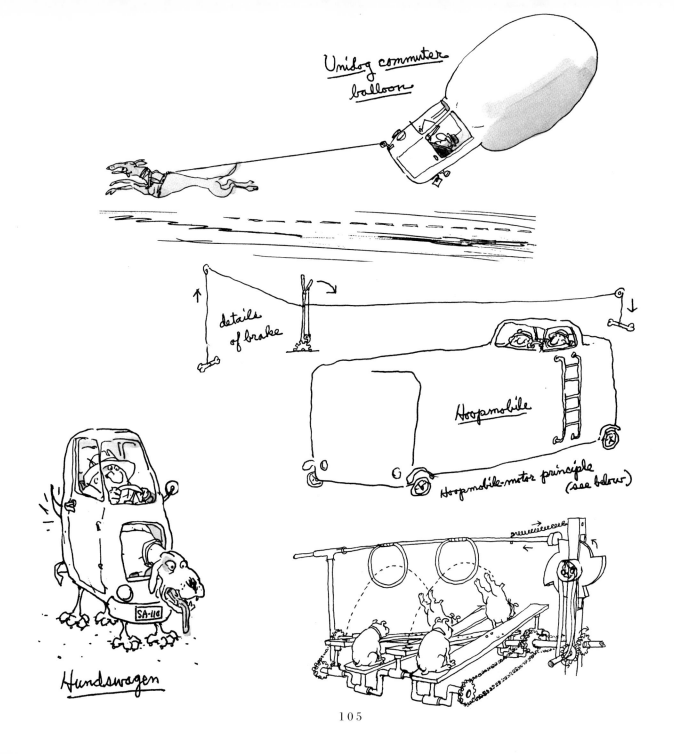

Unidog commuter balloon

details of brake

Hoopmobile

Hoopmobile-motor principle
(see below)

Hundswagen

SA-110

Avoid overstimulation.

Reserve a few minutes each morning
to recall the halcyon days of youth.

KEEPING CALM

Spend more time alone.

Putter among the flowers before breakfast.

Take catnaps whenever you can.

Every now and then, drop a few dirty dishes in the disposal.

Stay single.

FARTHER AFIELD

O N BEING INTRODUCED to a cartoonist, the predictable response is "Great fun! And what do you do for a living?" In America, less so abroad, cartooning is considered an undemanding and harmless hobby —midway between speed-walking and building a model of the Verrazano Bridge with toothpicks. Unfortunately, the same question also touches an unpleasant truth: few cartoonists make enough money from their chosen profession to support themselves. Even the most prolific contributors to *The New Yorker* make less than entry-level software jockeys. Aside from the lucky few who have married above themselves, cartoonists are obliged to subsidize their careers by working in related areas. Advertising, greeting cards, and children's books are high on the list—George has tried them all and a few more.

COMIC STRIPS

BOOTH: I sold "Local Item" to the Universal Press Syndicate back in the mid-eighties. The strip ran for about a year and then we stopped it. People in the East liked it, and people in California loved it, but the people in the Midwest didn't get it at all.

Just before it folded, the Chicago *Tribune* polled its readers. About fifty percent didn't care for it, and fifty percent said, "It's different." I guess it was too close to real life to be funny.

Local Item:

by George Booth

Gloria Loudermilk was installed as new president of the Ace Tires and Rubber By-Products, St. Joseph, last Saturday evening. Mrs. Wilma Van Gundy was named Woman of the Tire Year. Opal Freet received a 15-year service button, first pearls went to Rosalee Batts. Ron Hooper, Morris Taylor, Ken Pyle and Doris Schooley received perfect attendance awards.

Local Item:

by George Booth

Opal Hooper has been seeing her doctor at Lamoni, Iowa, once a week chaperoned by her mother, Mrs. Blanche Hooper.

Local Item:

by George Booth

Reverend Luke Warhm preached an excellent sermon Sunday morning at United Methodist, Mercy. Dub Beeson reports there were 31 sinners in attendance. Charlotta Qualls sang a special accompanied by Mrs. Ona Snuggs at the organ. It was just awful.

ILLUSTRATED BOOKS FOR CHILDREN
AND OTHERS

LORENZ: The books you've done for children did very well, yet you've only done four. How come?

BOOTH: I never intended to get into children's books, but when somebody offers you a story that's good, you gotta do it. I felt that way about *Possum Come a-Knockin'* and *Ballymara Flood* and *It's Not My Turn to Look for Grandma.*

The other one I did was twenty-three years ago. It was by Dr. Seuss (Theo. LeSieg) and it's still around. The kids wear it out. It's called *Wacky Wednesday,* and it's a book full of mistakes. George Washington sitting on his horse backwards, or a fish sitting on a park bench with a line and pole attached to a man in the pond. A palm tree growing out of a toilet. Seuss did the rough layouts, but I did the drawings. And I did the sight gags, such as they are. It's funny, he influenced me. It looks more like Seuss than it does Booth.

LORENZ: Did you do the tints yourself, or did you just indicate them?

BOOTH: I did each color separately.

LORENZ: On overlays?

BOOTH: No. In different shades of black and white. It drives you crazy. I swore I'd never do it again.

A sampling of Booth's embellishments for *Wacky Wednesday.*

In 1979, Booth illustrated *1,001 Logical Laws, Accurate Axioms, Profound Principles, Trusty Truisms, Homey Homilies, Colorful Corollaries, Quotable Quotes and Rambunctious Ruminations for All Walks of Life*. In a series of ads in *The New Yorker*, John Peers, the formulator of Peers' Law ("The solution to a problem changes the nature of the problem") had invited readers to send along favorite homilies of their own. The responses were too good not to share. The resulting book is a treasury of folk wisdom—a cross between Monty Python and *Poor Richard's Almanack*.

Carson's Law:
It's better to be rich
and healthy than
poor and sick.

Schwartz's Observation:
Just because you're paranoid doesn't mean
you're not being followed.

Hart's Homily:
Virginity can be cured.

LORENZ: You also illustrated two books by the comedian Henry Morgan.

BOOTH: Henry was living in Toronto back in the seventies, and he wanted to do a dog book. He titled it *Dogs*.

LORENZ: He asked you to illustrate it?

BOOTH: Right. And then he moved to Cape Cod with his wife, Karen. Dione and Karen and Henry and I became quite good friends. It sort of surprised me, because I'd seen him on television and I didn't think I wanted to get near him. I felt he was too sharp-tongued to be a friend. I figured the wallpaper'd pop off when he talked, but he was sweet. He was a wonderful person, and I miss him.

LORENZ: Didn't you once tell me about something you created and gave to him?

BOOTH: He liked the chicken shoes in my spread called "Keeping Warm." My kid brother was a shoe cobbler in Missouri. He made a pair of real shoes, and my mother fashioned a rubber chicken head for each shoe so it was sticking out of the toe. We sent them to Henry. He got a kick out of it, but he didn't want to keep the whole thing, so he returned one shoe.

LORENZ: What a gent. Do you still have it?

BOOTH: I don't know where it is.

LORENZ: What was the second book?

BOOTH: *The Uncensored Letters of Loreeta Pernie.* We didn't make any money on either book, but I made a friend. I think Henry gave Gomp Weez too big a role in the Pernie book. It's Henry's fault.

The chicken shoes from "Keeping Warm."

Aspirin Dog (Moon Bayer) from *Dogs*, by Morgan and Booth.

KEEPING WARM

Hot-water tie.
Warm all day at the office.

Heated
BB boots.
← CORK
Sew canvas boots.
Slip on over shoes.
Fill with hot BBs.
BBs heat fast in an iron skillet.

On sunny cold days, carry clothes in suitcase and quickly pinch on kitchen-foil suit.
Turkey pan (foil $1.29) will work best for quick pinch-on cap.

Heated tire irons wrapped in towels can be carried under one's topcoat.

Face catnip comforter.

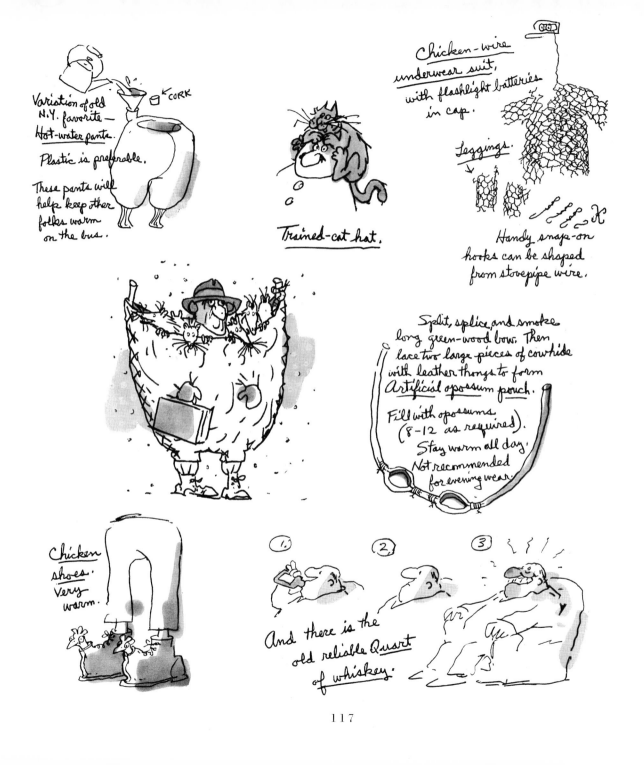

Variation of old N.Y. favorite — Hot-water pants.

Plastic is preferable.

These pants will help keep other folks warm on the bus.

← CORK

Trained-cat hat.

Chicken-wire underwear suit, with flashlight batteries in cap.

Leggings.

Handy snap-on hooks can be shaped from stovepipe wire.

Split, splice and smoke long green-wood bow. Then lace two large pieces of cowhide with leather thongs to form Artificial opossum pouch.

Fill with opossums (8-12 as required).

Stay warm all day. Not recommended for evening wear.

Chicken shoes. Very warm.

1. 2. 3.

And there is the old reliable Quart of whiskey.

117

GREETING CARDS

LORENZ: You did a successful series of greeting cards for Drawing Board.

BOOTH: That was in the late seventies. I worked with a lady named Jimmy Fitzgerald. We were a team. She did all the ideas, and I did all the line drawings. I would do a black-and-white drawing and send it to her in Texas. The art department would put on the color. I'd do about sixteen cards at once. The art director oversaw each job. It ran for a few years, then the mergers of the eighties changed the people and the setup.

I enjoyed my time with Jimmy and Drawing Board. Everything rolled along nicely. Fitzgerald and I hit it off pretty well, and sure enough, she was from Missouri.

Scratchings by BOOTH.

"DOING THE BATCH"

BOOTH: I like working on all this other stuff, but doing those weekly submissions for *The New Yorker* is what really matters. You probably feel the same way. It's an art that has developed in our lives to a degree that nothing else has. I feel sorry for writers. They put ten years in a book, they get a rejection, and it kills them. You and I get rejected or accepted every week, and then you see your work in print. There's nothing else so satisfying.

Hope you get it together for a Merry Christmas!

"By the way, HarperCollins decided your book did not warrant publication."

SHOPTALK

THE LATE PHILOSOPHER Sir Isaiah Berlin once remarked that "Shop talk is the best talk." Even if the shop is not your own, few things are more engrossing than hearing people talk about what matters most to them. George Booth is both a writer and an artist. This may seem self-evident, but in fact up until the sixties most of the cartoons that ran in *The New Yorker,* and elsewhere, were collaborations between artists and writers. Some of *The New Yorker*'s most familiar cartoonists—Arno, Hokinson, Whitney Darrow—relied heavily on gagmen. (Arno got many of his best ideas from James Geraghty, who later became art editor.) George Price, an unsurpassed draftsman, in fact never originated a single cartoon idea over his long, productive career.

CAPTIONS

Writing gags is a special talent, related more to writing for the stage or films than to writing comic prose. Many writers both on and off the *New Yorker* staff have tried their hand at creating cartoon ideas, but few have succeeded. Even Peter DeVries, who for ten years was himself a very reliable gag doctor at *The New Yorker* and the creator of brilliant comic novels, was rarely successful.

LORENZ: Cartooning is also writing, and a good cartoonist has to be a good writer.

BOOTH: Look at S.J. Perelman, who did cartoons before he became a writer.

LORENZ: Tell me about your approach to captions.

BOOTH: Well, with a caption like "Mrs. Van Lewis-Smythe, third wife of your chairman of the board . . ." I happened to read a pamphlet about fixing things in the home. A current subject was about the executive going to work daily while the wife was left with the drudgery of home. His life was a cinch, hers was a nightmare, so there was the direction of an idea.

LORENZ: That caption is wonderful. It's a soliloquy right up there with Molly Bloom.

BOOTH: It becomes a musical thing, a rhythm of writing and feeling. People do it different ways, I suppose. Generally I'm alone. I'll start to read it out loud, and get a feel for it and change it. I'll write all over three pages to get something like this, and then go back with a yellow marker and pick up parts of it and throw others out. It's a little bit like a poem. You get a feeling that rolls and then finally you get a punch. You may not know what it is while you're doing it, but you keep feeding . . .

LORENZ: Well, it's a very special kind of skill. Very few writers can do that.

BOOTH: It's like throwing corn to the chickens. You know, you get one chicken and after a while they all come around.

"Mrs. Van Lewis-Smythe, third wife of your chairman of the board,
said to me this evening at the corporate hoodingy, and twenty people within earshot,
'We all know what <u>Mr.</u> Parmalee does. He is a very important vice-president
of the Hi Lee Lolly Corporation. What we are all wondering, Mrs. Parmalee, is . . .
just what is it that <u>you</u> do? Do you do anything?' I said, 'Mrs. Van Lewis-Smythe,
Your Grace, I fix dripping faucets around our house. I prop up sagging bookshelves.
I glue broken china. I clean windows, mirrors, floors, walls, pots and pans,
and dishes. I jiggle the doodads on running toilets. I repair and refinish furniture.
I cane chairs. I paint and sew. I do electrical work, drive nails, saw boards,
and I give birth to our babies. I wash and iron and make the beds. I prepare the
meals. I get the children to school. I trim the hedge, plant and maintain a vegetable
garden and flower garden. I mow the lawn, clean the basement, feed the birds,
the cats, a dog, and a chicken, <u>and</u> I chauffeur a very important vice-president of the
Hi Lee Lolly Corporation to and from the bar car every blessed day.' "

"*The air I breathe is filthy, my food is poisoned, my automobile is a gas-guzzling behemoth, my school taxes have doubled, the Internal Revenue Service plans to take the fillings out of my teeth, my wife is fifty-three and pregnant, my dog bit a lawyer's kid, my son steals, my mother-in-law is a Communist, my daughter ran off with a fink, and now you tell me that if I don't back up and let you have the right-of-way I'll be in trouble.*"

"*Mother sends Season's Greetings with her love to you, Lydia. She says how she does so wish to spend the holidays with us but she knows that would mean we would have to drive five hundred and fifty miles to her house, as it is impossible for her to accept our invitation to come to our house, since our house, being so untidy, no offense intended, in parentheses, makes her uncomfortable to the point of actually causing her to become physically ill, but that she is willing to be a martyr all alone in order to keep everybody happy, while at the same time she is hoping with all the strength her aged bones can muster that we shall decide to drive to her house, knowing every mile of the five hundred and fifty miles that we are helping to make an old lady's heart very happy happy happy.*"

"Our main bank is right near your home, and we have fifteen other handy branches with all the latest push-button systems. We'll give you top interest rates and lollipops on your 'rainy-day' savings account. You can also have a safe-deposit box that no one but you is allowed to open. You'll get free 'stop-and-bank' souvenirs, such as little silver Empire State Buildings and Abraham Lincolns. There is a brand-new playground next to your bank, and you'll get a chance to win one of the grand sweepstakes prizes—hi-fi stereo, color television, or two weeks for two in Mexico City."

"It was Saturday night. The clock on my office wall showed the time to be eleven-forty-five. There are times when a private eye does not necessarily feel like being a private eye. This was one of those times. The elevator door down the hall clanked open with a clank familiar to anyone on the fourth floor who had had an office on the fourth floor as long as I had had an office on the fourth floor. Footsteps came down the darkened hall and stopped outside my door. They were the footsteps of a woman. . . ."

IDEAS

There are as many methods of creating cartoon ideas as there are cartoonists. Some free-associate wildly, hoping something will coalesce from the resulting mulch. Others patiently contemplate the blank paper on the drawing table, hoping that the Muse will take pity on them. Almost all use weekly magazines and daily papers to get the juices flowing. Flipping through cartoon anthologies is considered a legitimate form of stimulation. And if all else fails, there are always the old standbys—the couple on the desert island, the cavemen, the dragon and the fair maiden. I have never known an artist to seek inspiration from the files of his or her own previously published work. This confirms Picasso's famous dictum: "An artist is free to imitate anyone but himself."

LORENZ: How do you get your ideas? Do you read a lot, do you go to the movies, do you watch television?

BOOTH: I don't go to the movies much. I read a lot—that's how I get my timely stuff. Sometimes I get inspiration from just one word. Sometimes it's just walking down the street. It's being alive. It's remembering. I find that I can

draw a single tree that I looked at when I was nine years old. Or my father's 1925 Model T—I can still draw it in detail!

GAGMEN

The skewed vision that can turn even a mediocre draftsman into a comic artist is an equally rare phenomenon. Up to the mid-twenties, comic art was generally rendered in a bland, illustrative manner. The emergence at *The New Yorker* of bold stylists like Peter Arno and, later, George Price revolutionized the idea of what comic art could be. Though still based on solid draftsmanship, their work moved beyond that to something much more personal and involving. This set the stage for the great comic stylists, from Thurber and Addams to Saul Steinberg and Roz Chast.

BOOTH: Some years back, I would accept ideas from idea men and stick them up over my board because they were sharp ideas. Then when I'd sit down to work, I'd procrastinate on those ideas because I wanted to do my own. I discovered then that writing and drawing have to go together. The joy is in doing the whole thing. I do take an idea once in a while, but mostly when people ask me about it I say, "No, I do all my own stuff."

*"Lots of folks say the Reagan program is going to make a clean sweep
of all our problems right away, but Mr. Pudney has stated that it will be
quite some time yet before we get things licked into shape."*

"Attention, please, Mr. Lyle Ferguson. As a result of equipment failure at the Cos Cob power station, your train will not be running at all tonight."

"On my way home today on the bus, a lone grape rolled down the aisle and came to rest near my foot. It was pale green and looked to be of the seedless variety."

"By Jupiter, an angel! Or, if not, an earthly paragon!"

"The jackdaws are picking at my very heart!"

"Harmon was shaving and his stomach fell into the sink."

SIGHT GAGS

Sight gags are multipaneled, uncaptioned cartoon sequences. Every cartoonist has done a few, and some made it a specialty. The late Otto Soglow created "The Little King," which was a feature in *The New Yorker*'s early days and grew so popular that it became a syndicated comic strip and then a series of animated shorts. The undisputed master of this form, however, was Sam Cobean, whose work shone brilliantly but briefly at *The New Yorker* in the mid-forties. (He died in an auto accident in 1951.) Cobean began his career as a storyboard artist at Disney, and the influence of animation on his work is immediately apparent. Many of Cobean's sequences ran on for a dozen panels or more, and an inordinate number of them concerned men mentally undressing women. In Booth's sequences, the roles that Cobean assigned to oversexed males are distributed among chronically undernourished canines.

LORENZ: I miss those wonderful sequences you used to do. You mentioned Cobean. Cobean is one of the great forgotten masters of this form.

BOOTH: He was outstanding.

LORENZ: Some of your sequences remind me of those fifteen-minute shorts by Buster Keaton or Chaplin, full of elaborate sight gags.

BOOTH: You're hitting it. I was terribly influenced by those guys, and the Marx Brothers, too.

LORENZ: It's a great American tradition out of the silent films.

BOOTH: It's missing today.

LORENZ: Well, we seem to be talking about a lot of stuff that doesn't exist anymore.

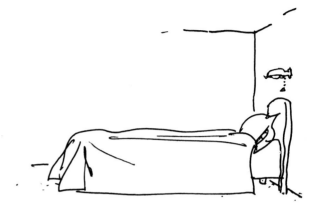

TECHNIQUE

Strictly speaking, a technique is just a tool, a means to an end. In fact, the tools particular artists choose often define their work for the public. Arno wasn't Arno until he threw away his charcoal sticks and began drawing with a loaded brush. Addams wasn't Addams until he mastered the difficult art of half-tone wash. And Saxon became Saxon when he put aside his crow quill pens and began drawing more directly with Wolff pencils. The best comic artists have created styles that most perfectly express their ideas. A Robert Weber cartoon rendered in the delicate pen line of Roz Chast would be as disappointing as a Chast drawing done with Bob Weber's charcoal sticks. Booth's style evolved slowly during his eight years at *Leatherneck*. At one time or another, he tried just about everything. His mature style, a carefully rendered pen sketch highlighted with half-tone, was in place by 1969, when he began publishing in *The New Yorker*.

BOOTH: I once got a proposal of marriage from a fan in the Midwest. She said, "Drop everything, even if you're married. We can work it out. I know you're no spring chicken by your shaky line."

LORENZ: Your roughs are covered with paste-ups. That's not unheard-of at *The New Yorker*, but you have developed it into a kind of fine art.

BOOTH: I started using pieces of invisible tape instead of glue. That probably drove the editors crazy, but the fact was when the camera took a picture of it, the tape created shadows like a piece of abstract art. I got a kick out of that.

Booth's unique use of invisible tape is illustrated by this drawing for *The New York Times* (August 9, 1998).

LORENZ: You didn't always work in ballpoint pen, obviously, because there weren't ballpoint pens when you started.

BOOTH: No, I worked with a brush and a crow quill, and later with a straight pen. You know, like an old-fashioned writing pen.

LORENZ: You also do something else that no one else does as far as I know, and that is, you put the half-tone on the back of the paper.

BOOTH: Yeah, with Magic Markers. I let it soak through.

LORENZ: Where did you pick that up?

BOOTH: Just from experimenting. If you get a good paper, the ink from the marker will soak through, and you get a softer edge than you can get if you do it on the front side of the drawing.

LORENZ: In a way, it gives you a very painterly effect.

BOOTH: It gives dimension to it. That's what I meant about the tape— it leaves a triangular shadow. Because I put half-tone on the back, it doesn't accidentally leave any lines where it crosses the tape. I prefer controlled accidents. If you don't have any accidents at all, it's kind of dull, really.

LORENZ: When you turn it over to do that, do you use a light table? Or can you still see the drawing?

BOOTH: I just look at it, and see where it is, and look at it like that and hit it with the black back here, and the black will soak through and make a dark spot.

"Ooooooh, just what I wanted!"

"*If you are fifty-five or older, you are liable at any moment to come completely unglued. Please call us, at the Glue Mutual Insurance Company. That's Glue. G-L-U-E. The Glue Mutual Insurance Company, at 800-176-5388. Now!*"

LORENZ: So there is a subtlety that you can't get if you apply it directly. When did you first come up with that, do you remember?

BOOTH: Early seventies. Or mid-seventies.

LORENZ: What did you do before that for half-tones, just use some wash?

BOOTH: Yes, I used to lay India ink washes, one over another. Seems archaic, doesn't it?

WORK HABITS

BOOTH: I tend to work all the time. Whatever else I'm doing, my head is there. I'm never happier than when I'm cartooning, and the more I accomplish, the better. I'm very slow. I'm awfully slow. I tend to be a night person.

My background contains a lot of discipline. I got drafted into the Marine Corps, and I have a feeling for discipline and being on time. As a result, I try to put my rear end in the chair at nine A.M. Not that I'm always ready to work, but it helps me to get there.

"The wattle fairy came again last night."

"This is my son Sam, the doctor; my son Winston, the lawyer;
and my son Alden, the lawnblower."

"Good news, Mr. Herndon. We worked out the budget, and we have a kidney."

"First you must see Dr. Ta, and then you must see Dr. Ra Ra, and after that you may see Dr. Boom T. Ay."

INFLUENCES

LORENZ: Aside from your parents, who would you say has had the greatest impact on your life and the direction of your work?

BOOTH: Dione, my wife, has been a major influence. We married in 1958. She and her family introduced me to the cat world. Dione supported my career and still does. She's a musician, knows plants and flowers, and is well-read on many subjects—she's one of those self-taught people whereby education continues. Mother was like that. I was blessed with marrying into a wonderful family.

Murel Crawford, my agriculture teacher in high school, encouraged my cartooning. Agriculture was mandatory, but he knew I never intended to be a farmer.

Thinking about it, I realize I cannot list all the good people who have been an influence and helpful along the way. They all become major. Dione has a broad knowledge of music and keeps us nourished in that part of life. We heard a lot of jazz in New Orleans when daughter Sarah lived there. Right now I'm doing covers for some jazz CDs.

Barbara Nicholls (Nicholls Gallery) introduced us to George Price and Charles Addams. She invited us to George's ninetieth birthday party in New Jersey. He walked me out to the back and showed me his barn. That is memorable to me.

Dione and Barbara and I were out at Charles and Tee Addams' in Bridgehampton. Charles showed us his 1921 racer car. He explained that all cars of that

*"Mama and I fixed a lovely dinner. I used the right side of my brain,
and she used the left side of her brain."*

"I've got an idea for a story: Gus and Ethel live on Long Island, on the
North Shore. He works sixteen hours a day writing fiction. Ethel never goes out,
never does anything except fix Gus sandwiches, and in the end she becomes
a nympho-lesbo-killer-whore. Here's your sandwich."

model were painted a certain blue. He had had it painted a flat black because he thought it looked better. We decided it was warmer.

Charles Saxon was a gem of a man. I never knew Sam Cobean; he was another excellent cartoonist. Henry Martin, William Steig, Mischa Richter, Shel Silverstein, C.E. Martin, Frank Modell, Saul Steinberg, Helen Hokinson, Peter Arno, Dorothy Parker added to the hopper.

I was influenced by the work of Fred Lasswell ("Snuffy Smith"), Ralph Stein (magazines and newspaper work), Karl Hubenthal (political), Bill Mauldin, Fontaine Fox, Thomas Nast, Fred Opper, Rudolph Dirks, Laurel and Hardy, the Marx Brothers, George McManus, Herriman ("Krazy Kat"), J.R. Williams, Vincent van Gogh, Frank Willard, Segar, Walt Disney, Milton Caniff. Alley Oop comics impressed me. Oh, these cartoonists were so wonderful. Adolph Knerr. Katzenjammer Kids. Mutt and Jeff.

I am a Bill Cosby fan. There is an outstanding man.

Toulouse-Lautrec! Matisse! Miró! Buster Keaton! Prof. Ken Hine of Syracuse!

Did I mention Mary Petty?

Vaudeville!

—*G.B.*

"Hudson, about our reservations at the Rainbow Room
for the millennium—I raffled them off."

ADVICE

BOOTH: The best advice I ever got was from my mother. I was nine years old and I was giving my first chalk talk. I was too shy to say anything, so she talked while I drew. When I was done, I sat down like a shot. Mother practically tore my shirt off making me stand up to take a bow. She said, "You stand up there and act like you know something, whether you do or not!"

She was also a great believer in "stick-to-itiveness." Some people think to be a cartoonist you have to be angry. I never understood that. I don't believe in throwing a snot fit every five minutes. Just act like you know something, stick to it, and—one more thing Mother said—give it plenty of "oomph."

" 'The difference <u>you</u> make makes <u>all</u> the difference.' Well put!"

A BOOTH
BIBLIOGRAPHY

COLLECTIONS OF CARTOONS BY GEORGE BOOTH

THINK GOOD THOUGHTS ABOUT A PUSSYCAT.
Dodd, Mead & Company, 1975.

REHEARSAL'S OFF!
Dodd, Mead & Company, 1976.

PUSSYCATS NEED LOVE, TOO.
Dodd, Mead & Company, 1980.

OMNIBOOTH: THE BEST OF GEORGE BOOTH.
Congdon & Weed, Inc., 1984.

BOOTH AGAIN!
Andrews & McMeel, 1989.

BOOKS ILLUSTRATED BY GEORGE BOOTH

Theo. LeSieg, WACKY WEDNESDAY.
Random House, Inc., 1974.

Henry Morgan and George Booth, DOGS.
Houghton Mifflin Company, 1976.

John Peers and Gordon Bennett, eds., 1,001 Logical Laws,
Accurate Axioms, Profound Principles, Trusty Truisms,
Homey Homilies, Colorful Corollaries, Quotable Quotes,
and Rambunctious Ruminations for All Walks of Life.
Doubleday, 1979.

Henry Morgan, The Uncensored Letters of Loreeta Pernie:
Bought for Three Dollars in a Garage Sale.
Congdon & Weed, Inc., 1982.

Nancy Van Laan, Possum Come a-Knockin'.
Alfred A. Knopf, Inc., 1990.

Chad Stuart, The Ballymara Flood: A Tale from Old Ireland.
Harcourt Brace Jovanovich, Inc., 1995.

April Halprin Wayland, It's Not My Turn to Look for Grandma.
Alfred A. Knopf, Inc., 1995.

SELECTED DRAWINGS BY GEORGE BOOTH

The New Yorker Album of Drawing, 1925–1975.
Viking Press, 1978.

The New Yorker Cartoon Album, 1975–1985.
Viking Press, 1985.

Lee Lorenz, ed., The Art of The New Yorker.
Alfred A. Knopf, Inc., 1995.

GEORGE BOOTH is, paradoxically, a late bloomer who started drawing "funny pictures" when he was three but didn't begin his thirty-year association with *The New Yorker* until he was in his forties. Mr. Booth got his professional start in the Marines while on the staff of *Leatherneck*, the USMC's official publication, and from there his work began to appear in *Collier's* and other periodicals. Booth was on the eve of breaking through in *The Saturday Evening Post* when it folded, with the ultimately happy result that Booth, like Charles Barsotti, was picked up by the *New Yorker* editor William Shawn. A self-described "corn belt" Missourian, Booth has never lost that certain Mark Twain flavor of small-town eccentricity. He lives with his wife, Dione, on Long Island.

LEE LORENZ, an acclaimed cartoonist, was art editor of *The New Yorker* from 1973 through 1993. Mr. Lorenz and his family live in western Connecticut.